TUMBLEWEED

Poems

by Kelly Johnston

BLUE
CEDAR
PRESS

Wichita, Kansas

TUMBLEWEED

Copyright 2021 by Kelly Johnston. All rights reserved. No part of this book may be reproduced or utilized in any manner whatsoever without written permission, except in the case of brief quotations embodied in critical articles and reviews. Inquiries should be addressed to:

Blue Cedar Press
P.O. Box 48715
Wichita, KS 67201

First edition.
10 9 8 7 6 5 4 3 2 1
ISBN: 978-1-7369112-3-5

Cover photo by Canva
Composition by Gina Laiso
Managing Editor, Laura Tillem

Acknowledgements
"Circles" was first published in *The I-70 Review,* Summer/Fall 2020
"In the Desert Near White Sands" was first published by the California State Poetry Society in the *California Quarterly,* Vol. 43, Number 3 (2017).

Printed in the United States of America

DEDICATION

Tumbleweed is dedicated to my mother, Colleen Kelly Johnston, who inspired me to read for enjoyment, to use my imagination, and to write creatively. She started me reading Louis L'Amour westerns, all of which I have read many times. She later suggested Tony Hillerman, C.J. Box and Dana Stabenow. She was also a creative writer and, for many years, I was unaware of her work. She participated in a critique group with writers Myrne Roe and the late Diane Wahto, both fine poets themselves, as well as my friends. I owe Mom so much more than this dedication.

AUTHOR'S NOTE

The title for this book of poetry comes from a Louis L'Amour novel, *Conagher*. In this novel, the protagonist, Conn Conagher, is a cowboy. While riding, he begins to find pieces of paper tied to tumbleweeds blowing across the prairie. On these pieces of faded paper are poems written by a lonely woman. Conagher wondered who the author was, and the story leads to conflict and love. You may remember a movie by the same name starring Sam Elliott and Katharine Ross. This book of poetry serves as the framework for the delivery by me to you of these poems. I have not yet tried tying some of my poems to tumbleweeds. Maybe soon. Maybe.

ABOUT THE AUTHOR

Kelly Johnston is a life-long Kansan, who was born in Lawrence in 1955. He graduated from Wichita Heights High School in 1973 and Wichita State University in 1977 with a creative writing major in the English Department. He studied under A.G. Sobin, Anita Skeen and L.M. Grow. He published poems while in college in *Mikrokosmos, The Cottonwood Review* and *The Ark River Review*. He then attended law school at KU, graduated in 1979, and then began practicing law for 42 years. Those lawyering years caused him to take a respite from creative writing, but he began writing seriously again in 2007. He has published poems more recently in *The I-70 Review, The Flint Hills Review* and *the California Quarterly*. His chapbook *Kalaska* was published by Blue Cedar Press in 2017. Kelly is married to LaDeena and they have three children, Shayla, Jaime and Brendan, and four grandchildren Mia, Kelly Jr., Reese and Henry. Kelly loves to spend time on his land in the Chautauqua Hills near Cross Timbers State Park, where many of his poems have been inspired.

Table of Contents

Prologue:
  Treasure Hunters / 2
Part One: Critters
  Crows at Night / 4
  Blackbirds / 5
  Monster of The Deep / 6
Part Two: People
  Twilight Rescue / 8
  Circles / 9
  The Game / 10
  Holding on to Hope of Spring / 11
  Replanting / 12
  My Walking Stick / 13
  Dad's Wallet / 14
  Relics / 15
  Mountains of Memories / 16
  Wasting Time / 17
Part Three: Places
  In the Desert Near White Sands / 20
  Fox Lake 1969 / 21
  In the Kansas Wilds / 22
  Prairie Ripples and Waves / 23
  Reacting to Darkness and Light / 24
  Weekend Respite / 25
  In the Canyons of the Anasazi / 26
  Last Scarlet Days of August / 27
Epilogue:
  Golden / 28

Prologue

Treasure Hunters

The campfire's soft glow –
moonlight glancing off golden
coins waiting to be found.

Old men huddled around fire:
teeth flash yellow while telling stories
of treasure, and the monsters that guard.

Under leaves at firelight's perimeter,
scorpions discuss ways to capture prey:
 "Humans are attracted to light, they say.
Yes, like to beer and gold."
They wait until men fall into final stupor.
Scorpions surround their victims.

Pale bodies now filled with venom,
scorpions plunder pockets and packs.
to gloat over their victory,
to fondle their golden coins.

Part One: Critters

Crows at Night

I have never heard a crow at night.
From roosts on bone-white arms
of sycamore and birch, crows rustle
feathers like leaves and lift moonward.

I know where they are at sunrise.
Crow soldiers constantly call
the murder. When I hike to the ridge,
they announce my march like reveille.

I have never seen a crow at night.
They are obsidian shards cast across
the night sky. When starlight glints off
their feathers, a meteor shower appears.

The murder glides low on the horizon
and disappears into the tallgrass
for prey, except for one sentinel
I cannot see or hear but know is there
waiting a turn at the bone pile.

Red-Winged Blackbirds

The prairie fire makes skeletons
of a grove of red cedars, reduces
to ash tallgrass and wildflowers,
reveals rusty strands of barbed wire
suturing the wounded ground.

My chainsaw makes short work of bones.
Splinters and shards scrape and gouge
my flesh. Dripping blood nourishes
scorched earth and blackened stubble.
We wait for replenishing rains
with red-winged blackbirds.

Monster of the Deep

He rows across the lake at midnight.
Oar locks rattle and groan as paddles
slip through the glassy surface, nudging
aside reflections of stars and crescent moon.
A bait bucket sloshes, a head lamp pierces,
a hand slaps a mosquito hunting for blood.
Somewhere a skunk has panicked.

At last, he locates the trotline.
Hand over hand, he pulls the boat down
the line, finds each hook shiny and bare,
until he feels a heaviness ahead, moving
away, and he begins to hope, until the mossy
head of a huge snapper breaks water.
He drops the net, fumbles at his side
for the holster, cocks and shoots
the monster in the head. He cuts the line
and watches the carcass sink into the abyss.
Only a film of blood and bubbles remain.

Though the creel hangs empty beside the boat,
each hook is rebaited, placed three feet deep,
and the next journey before dawn dreamed.

Part Two: People

Twilight Rescue
For Brendan

Amid the silt of a retreating river,
an egret is motionless in the mud.
River bottom grime has stained
wing tips and belly down.
Spindle legs disappear in the muck.
Long neck and head rotate like radar.

The skinny boy is shirtless,
white washboard ribs vivid.
He steps off the bank, sinks in
to his ankles, wobbles to gain balance,
drags one boot free and steps forward.
The egret watches, trembles,
tries again to escape.

The boy whispers like an angel,
bends from the waist as his legs
are clutched by the mud.
One finger traces a line along
the bird's back, neck and crest
then grabs the beak. The other
arm cradles the egret, raises
it out of the mud and into flight –
moonrise from horizon's misery.

Circles

A drake and hen mallard, their journey
to Canada briefly delayed, disturb
the icy edge of the spring-fed pond.
No vultures are on death patrol yet.
They stay somewhere south waiting
for bald eagles to leave. Robins
flash crimson among bare branches.
Steam rises from my coffee mug.

As the crescent moon arcs toward
the west horizon, and the sun follows
a similar arc, sugar maples are budding,
daffodils are showing golden heads.
Redbuds are still asleep though. Bluets
and rose verbena are just a dream.

In short-sleeves by late afternoon,
I cast a spinner into the shallows
on the west shoreline where sunshine
warms the water soonest. Two bass
are deceived and landed. A sharp knife
and deft cuts result in four filets.
I toss the remains to the turtles.

I sip cabernet and imagine a garden
of sunset-colored Indian blanket.
It has been a long winter, but chorus
frogs are announcing the return of spring.
Half of summer I will give to mowing
to try to keep ticks and poison ivy at bay,
and to avoid searching for grandchildren
lost in fields of big bluestem and sumac.

The Game

His belly adds another ring as
her eyes retreat into hollow pits.
He watches the Packers while
recalling the barrage on opening day
of goose season, the debates about who
was the killer, and taunts about prowess
with shotguns and women.

She prepares to clean the game.
Spits on whetstone, strokes knife
like caressing a pet. She
grasps the long cold neck, slices
from ass to wishbone, removes
the head. She smiles as the cavities
fill, and he smiles as the Packers score.

Holding on to Hope of Spring

I hear the north wind carrying
icy messages from high country.
Oaks cling to last year's leaves.
Redbuds have not yet purpled.
Bluets have not yet peeked.

Static erupts from my blankets
as I reach for a split of firewood.
The winter wood pile is almost gone.
My trailer door rattles in unison
with skeletons of burnt cedars
resisting the wind. Turkey vultures
have returned to resume the wait.
Pulling my boots over worn woolen
socks is a chore. The floor is a glacier.

I tire of reusing coffee grounds.
If my truck will start, I must
journey south for provisions.
Maybe I will find fescue greening
in short grass beside the road, or henbit
taking over winter wheat. Even a golden
dandelion emerging from the dust,
like the sun from the horizon,
would be a sign.

Replanting

My garden in the Chautauqua Hills
is bordered by shards of sandstone
reddened by eons of exposure
to iron water. Each stone I discovered
in tallgrass, or protruding from exposed
soil, or resting on a talus slope.
Each stone was relocated
to carefully assembled walls.
I transplanted day lilies and iris
from the city into the garden. Hardy
reliable bloomers, they fail to spark
fire like prairie wild rose, butterfly weed,
blazing star or Indian blanket.

One day when my energy joins the cosmos,
my ashes will be transplanted
among the flowers. My elements will
merge with roots, worms and mushrooms.
I will smile in blazing colors.

In a few generations, oak forest may
reclaim the garden. Distant kin may forget
my planting, but I will continue to circulate
in the rainfall, hedge apples, oak trees,
squirrel and deer scat. Each turn of spring
will feature every flower, commanded
by warmth of soil, or angle of sunlight,
to take turn at pollination.
I will be blowing in the wind.

My Walking Stick

I rescued a sycamore sapling
from the lake. Beavers had stripped it
smooth but left it floating in the froth.
My hand fit firmly around it.

My walking stick serves as a third leg
on rocky slopes, allows me to rustle
piles of oak leaves bunched behind roots
or shards of sandstone where a copperhead
might be sunning. From a distance
it might appear as if I were blind.

It moves aside poison ivy, checks
a turtle carapace for life, or probes
the depths of the creek feeding the lake.
I proudly show it off to the beavers
as I pass their den each day.

Dad's Wallet

He taught me to be a gentleman
but would not offer a hand
in his last years. Many possessions
heirs debated and divided. His
wallet I had been holding awhile.

The leather is cracked by decades
of sunshine sitting on the tray
by the tennis court waiting
for the end.

The stitching is frayed and loose
from countless pocketed hours.
Pigment is bruised and purpled
from sunscreen and sweat.

When mine was stolen,
I emptied it of a red-white-blue
Medicare card, an expired driver's license,
and a stained photo of him and his Dad
at enlistment.

I now notice how easily
my skin is gouged and bloodied.

Relics

As I count off the last minutes
of shooting time after sundown,
undulating waves of big bluestem hide
movements of whitetail deer. If lucky,
I might still see yellowed antlers moving
along the grassy skyline like a harrier,
or a flash of white as a doe guides
her fawn away from danger.

I have hunted this land for decades,
as did those who came before. I never
find their bone piles, fire rings or prints.
Only flinty points, or a grain grinder.
Their ghosts still chase buffalo
across the wild Kansas skies. Fires
used to push a herd over a cliff
still burn every spring.

When the tallgrass of last
year has turned to ash, relics
of more recent peoples are found:
forgotten cisterns like
portals to Hades, a line of sandstone
blocks that founded a settler's home,
flattened beer cans and shards
of glass cast aside by a previous owner.
My empty shell casings I try to retrieve.

In the haze beyond my days,
the two-track cut across this land
will be overgrown. Deer and coyotes
and maybe a cougar or black bear
will find refuge. My flesh and bones
will decay and join the soil, leaving
my belt buckle or a coin
to be found by a distant hunter.

Mountains of Memories

I drove alone into the Rockies.
At a roadside brook,
acquainted my feet with glacial water,
arrested my pulse.

I found a sheet of mica,
peered through at the sun,
put it in my pocket
next to my heart.

I kicked a pinecone down
a trail beside the Big Thompson,
talked back to a robber jay,
wondered whether a grizzly
was waiting ahead.

Though I have not returned,
I can see the blue spires
on the horizon drawing me near,
smell the spruce and pine,
feel the reliable afternoon,
hear a mountain lion scream
in the cliffs ahead.

I dream of wet feet, diffuse light
and mysteries of the wild.

Wasting Time

The light is still dim around
the edge of the curtain.
A bobwhite quail's three-note
call close by disturbs me.
I drag myself from the depths
of slumber, try to remember
what day it is.

Last night, Neowise finally arrived
after six thousand years of dawdling.
I sat on the deck for hours sipping
wine, slapping mosquitos and yelling
at 'dillos to stay out of my garden.
Someday, another Ice Age will send
them south with the rest of the climate
invaders. I will continue to wait and dream.

Humans finally emerged from Africa
but Lucy could have spent less time
on her knuckles. Neanderthals could
have waved the white flag sooner.
If so, perhaps we would not still be
polluting the planet. I must wait
and wait for another Enlightenment.
Maybe to come from the East again
with Siddhartha and the rising sun.

I think I know how much wood to cut
to get through the night. Will need
to catch a fish or two for supper. Soon,
the frayed threads of day will storm
into the black hole of sleep,
conglomerate into a breccia
of anxiety and paranoia.
The gravity of darkness pulls
me into sediment I may not be
able to escape. I hope I hear
soon outside my window the
quail calling me to emerge.

Part Three: Places

In the Desert Near White Sands

Canyon slopes are sharp,
covered with loose rock,
cholla and agave.
Mule deer lie in the shade
of juniper and mesquite.
We try to make them rise and run.

Scattering stones alert us:
rifles fire, spent shells clatter,
bolts seat another round,
echoes fade downslope.
Later, dusk ebbs the wind,
quail rustle the sand,
silence settles in.

Around the campfire,
we talk of the canyons
to hunt tomorrow,
deer we missed today,
women we only knew.

The night air turns crisp,
the campfire smolders,
and bedrolls beckon.
Far away, a missile rises
from White Sands silent.
We watch the stages separate
as our jaws slacken, wonder
what is in the air.

Fox Lake 1969

Fishing under a full moon,
I wade in the black hole of a still
lake. Mud seizes me at each step.
Silt eddies behind into history.
Extra tackle is stowed on my vest,
glasses and spotlight strapped to head.
I am tethered to a bleeding minnow
writhing down deep, trying to escape
blood trail drifting down current.

I wait for the future beneath the moon
where Armstrong is tied to lunar lander,
oxygen flowing into helmet, radio
into space. Feeling my line for a tap,
I imagine each moment of movement,
moonscape reflected in face shield, flag
unfurled without wind. Footprints
at base of ladder never fade.

In the Kansas Wilds

Most of us know the squeal of tires
or squeaking of brakes at night,
but I have heard the long slow
hoot of the Great Horned Owl,
the chatter of raccoons feeding
in lake shallow, the echoing calls
of whippoorwills drifting in the forest,
and hundreds of feet and wings of geese
churning the lake surface to take flight.

Most of us know the blare of TV
discussing news of yesterday,
but I have heard the gobble at dawn
of a bearded tom protecting his flock,
the splash of a bass attacking a frog
trying to skip to the safety of shore,
and the snort of a whitetail buck catching
my scent as I pass on a morning hike.

Most of us know the anxious dreams
that awaken us too early,
but I have taken the hand of a child,
and turned over rocks and logs to find
a red scorpion or a collared snake
or a hairy wolf spider, and I have
picked wild blackberries and laughed
as my grandson purpled his face and hands.
I have seen in my granddaughter's eyes
the azure sky reflected in the lake.

Prairie Ripples and Waves

Rainfall pierces the worn canvas of my tent.
Huddled beneath blankets, I watch hillside
seeps become rivulets, lap over my floor,
soak my bedding, and float inside
bits of bark, acorn husks, and old leaves.

Outside, the lake spillway gushes
with limbs and logs, beer cans at crest.
Creek banks downstream cave and crash
into frothy torrent. An oak tree loses
hold of rocky soil and slides into Hades.
A hasty retreat I must make.

I awaken safe in my truck.
Doves mourn. A doe and fawn
hesitantly test the still steady flow
of muddy water. Like bone revealed
by laceration, a new shelf of sandstone
emerges from the bank. Ancient
ripple marks see sunlight once again.

Reacting to Darkness and Light

Dawn has breached the horizon
but darkness remains unmoved.
In the mystery of slumber,
we need sunshine in our eyes.

Outside, lightning strobes
expose top leaves of blackjack oak
bending to the wind. Branches
of Osage Orange writhe
and stretch parallel to ground.
Persimmon trees thrive narrow
and tall on the edge of the forest.
We struggle against the inertia
of dream-state.

Copperheads wait under rocks
for the forest floor to warm.
Grasshoppers hold tight to stems
while droplets evaporate from wings.
The dark space between us
yields to the merging of our lights
and the anxiety of night subsides.

Weekend Respite

July thunderheads blossom in the west.
Troubles blow through me with the gust front.
Deadlines extend beyond the horizon
like a rusty, sagging fence across these hills.

The hum of cicadas at twilight overwhelms
quail calling to covey for the night. Mourning
doves are graveling on the two-track. A bass
leaps at a dragonfly, splashes into the pond.
Friday evening dissolves the week behind.

When the Saturday sun brightens the west
ridge above the Verdigris River valley,
and the edge of day creeps east, again
I will try to contain nature by mowing,
edging and spraying. I will discover
new wildflower blossoms, others faded
and dead. I will fill in the holes dug by
armadillos, and notice the long-fingered,
delicate tracks of raccoons from last night.

If the lightning-latticed clouds on the horizon
give rain, we will start a fire, burn brush,
sip cold beer and send dreams aloft
on the wings of whippoorwills.

In the Canyons of the Anasazi

The wind stills at sundown. Quail rustle
the sand finding cover for the night.
Stars descend, blues fade black, bedrolls beckon.
A dim light across the valley defines the horizon.

Overnight, fog settles on the hills,
invades canyons painted with petroglyphs.
We knew the path to retrieve yesterday's kill,
having taken back to camp before sunset
only the head, cape and liver. Following
a sheep trail down sharp slopes amid clouds,
we give constant attention to loose rock,
agave and ocotillo. From the bottom, among
juniper and pinon, the hilltops are shrouded.
Each canyon looks the same. We have lost
the deer. We backtrack to camp, fry
liver and onions over mesquite.

A brief blizzard blows through the hills
encrusting cholla in ice. The sky is lapis
blue, the air crisp as a gunshot. Keeping
an eye on distinct hilltops, we find the muley,
cut carcass in half, tie each to a pack frame.
We haul the meat uphill and down, sweating
and gasping, break off crusts of ice for thirst.

We rest on slabs of limestone fallen from canyon
cliffs during an ancient thaw and freeze, find
pottery shards in the bunchgrass behind.

Last Scarlet Days of August

The low-water bridge is as dry as deer
bones tossed aside by turkey vultures.
Hedgerows are covered in limestone dust.
Big bluestem curves to constant south wind.
A solitary monarch butterfly searches.

Wildflowers have blossomed, wilted,
seeded since the prairie fire. Blazing star
and goldenrod are fading. Clouds
of grasshoppers billow ahead
of my boots. A few leaves of sumac
have started the autumn bleed.

The lake edges are stagnant. Isles
of blue-green algae are decaying
wounds. Not a fish or dragonfly
dimples the dead surface. Web
worms consume young oak and
sycamore branches. Around
the lake, cardinal plants are on fire.

Epilogue

Golden

The full moon breaks the horizon,
reflects in a placid spring-fed pond.
Raccoons chatter on the far shore
searching for shellfish in short water.
Mayfly nymphs struggle to rise
above foraging bass and bluegill.

Campfire embers drift toward
The Milky Way. Children sit close
to firepit rimrock, laugh with eyes
ablaze. Older eyes follow their hands
and feet, glimpse darting bats attracted
by bugs lured to death by golden light.

In the dark edges of night beyond
the cocoon of warmth, pairs of wild
luminescent eyes are golden coins
long ago dropped and forgotten
by Spaniards seeking Cibola.

www.ingramcontent.com/pod-product-compliance
Lightning Source LLC
Chambersburg PA
CBHW070038040426
42333CB00040B/1715